JOANN SEBASTIAN

BACH

24 PRELUDE AND FUGUE SHEET MUSIC

ISBN/SKU: 9781802210279

CONTENT

1. PRELUDE AND FUGUE IN C MAJOR BWV 846 - PAG. 3
2. PRELUDE AND FUGUE IN C MINOR BWV 847 - PAG. 8
3. PRELUDE AND FUGUE IN C# MAJOR BWV 848 - PAG. 13
4. PRELUDE AND FUGUE IN C# MINOR BWV 849 - PAG. 21
5. PRELUDE AND FUGUE IN D MAJOR BWV 850 - PAG. 28
6. PRELUDE AND FUGUE IN D MINOR BWV 851 - PAG. 33
7. PRELUDE AND FUGUE IN E-FLAT MAJOR BWV 852 - PAG. 38
8. PRELUDE AND FUGUE IN E-FLAT MINOR BWV 853 - PAG. 45
9. PRELUDE AND FUGUE IN E MAJOR BWV 854 - PAG. 52
10. PRELUDE AND FUGUE IN E MINOR BWV 855 - PAG. 57
11. PRELUDE AND FUGUE IN F MAJOR BWV 856 - PAG. 62
12. PRELUDE AND FUGUE IN F MINOR BWV 857 - PAG. 67
13. PRELUDE AND FUGUE IN F# MAJOR BWV 858 - PAG. 74
14. PRELUDE AND FUGUE IN F# MINOR BWV 859 - PAG. 79
15. PRELUDE AND FUGUE IN G MAJOR BWV 860 - PAG. 84
16. PRELUDE AND FUGUE IN G MINOR BWV 861 - PAG. 91
17. PRELUDE AND FUGUE IN A-FLAT MAJOR BWV 862 - PAG. 96
18. PRELUDE AND FUGUE IN G-SHARP MINOR BWV 863 - PAG. 101
19. PRELUDE AND FUGUE IN A MAJOR BWV 864 - PAG. 106
20. PRELUDE AND FUGUE IN A MINOR BWV 865 - PAG. 111
21. PRELUDE AND FUGUE IN B-FLAT MAJOR BWV 866 - PAG. 121
22. PRELUDE AND FUGUE IN B-FLAT MINOR BWV 867 - PAG. 126
23. PRELUDE AND FUGUE IN B MAJOR BWV 868 - PAG. 131
24. PRELUDE AND FUGUE IN B MINOR BWV 869 - PAG. 136

1. Prelude and Fugue in C major BWV 846

Part First.
Preludio I.

All figures in the fingering which are set above the notes are intended, whether in inner or outer parts, for the right hand; whereas, the figures below the notes are for the left hand. This explanation will suffice to show, in doubtful cases, by which hand any note in the inner parts is to be played.

Alle Fingersatz-Zahlen, welche über den Noten stehen, gelten (auch in den Mittelstimmen) stets der rechten Hand. Dagegen sind die unter den Noten stehenden Zahlen immer für die linke Hand bestimmt. Dieses reicht hin, um in zweifelhaften Fällen anzuzeigen, von welcher Hand jede Note in den Mittelstimmen gegriffen werden muss.

Fuga I.
a 4 Voci.

2. Prelude and Fugue in C minor BWV 847

Preludio II.

Allegro vivace. (♩= 144.)

Fuga II.
a 3 Voci.

3. Prelude and Fugue in C# major BWV 848

PRELUDE and FUGUE, in C♯ major
From the Well-tempered Clavichord

Edited by Moritz Moszkowski

JOHANN SEBASTIAN BACH
(1685 - 1750)

4. Prelude and Fugue in C# minor BWV 849

Preludio IV.

Andante con moto. (♩= 92)

Fuga IV.
a 5 Voci.

Moderato e maestoso. (♩ = 112)

5. Prelude and Fugue in D major BWV 850

Preludio V.

Allegro vivace. (♩ = 132)

Fuga V.
a 4 Voci.

Allegro moderato. (♩ = 76)

6. Prelude and Fugue in D minor BWV 851

Preludio VI.

Fuga VI.
a 3 Voci.

7.   Prelude and Fugue in E-flat major BWV 852

PRAELUDIUM VII.

FUGA VII.

8. Prelude and Fugue in E-flat minor BWV 853

Preludio VIII.

Fuga VIII.
a 3 Voci.

9.   Prelude and Fugue in E major BWV 854

Preludio IX.

Fuga IX.
a 3 Voci.

10. Prelude and Fugue in E minor BWV 855

Preludio X.

Allegro molto moderato. (♩=84.)

Fuga X.
a 2 Voci.

11. Prelude and Fugue in F major BWV 856

Preludio XI.

Fuga XI.
a 3 Voci.

12. Prelude and Fugue in F minor BWV 857

Preludio XII.

Fuga XII.
a 4 Voci.

Andante serioso. (♩ = 63.)

13.   Prelude and Fugue in F# major BWV 858

Preludio XIII.

Fuga XIII.
a 3 Voci.
Allegretto piacevole. (♩= 88.)

14. Prelude and Fugue in F# minor BWV 859

Preludio XIV.

Fuga XIV.
a 4 Voci.

15. Prelude and Fugue in G major BWV 860

Preludio XV.

Fuga XV.
a 3 Voci.

Allegretto vivace. (♩.=80.)

16. Prelude and Fugue in G minor BWV 861

Preludio XVI.

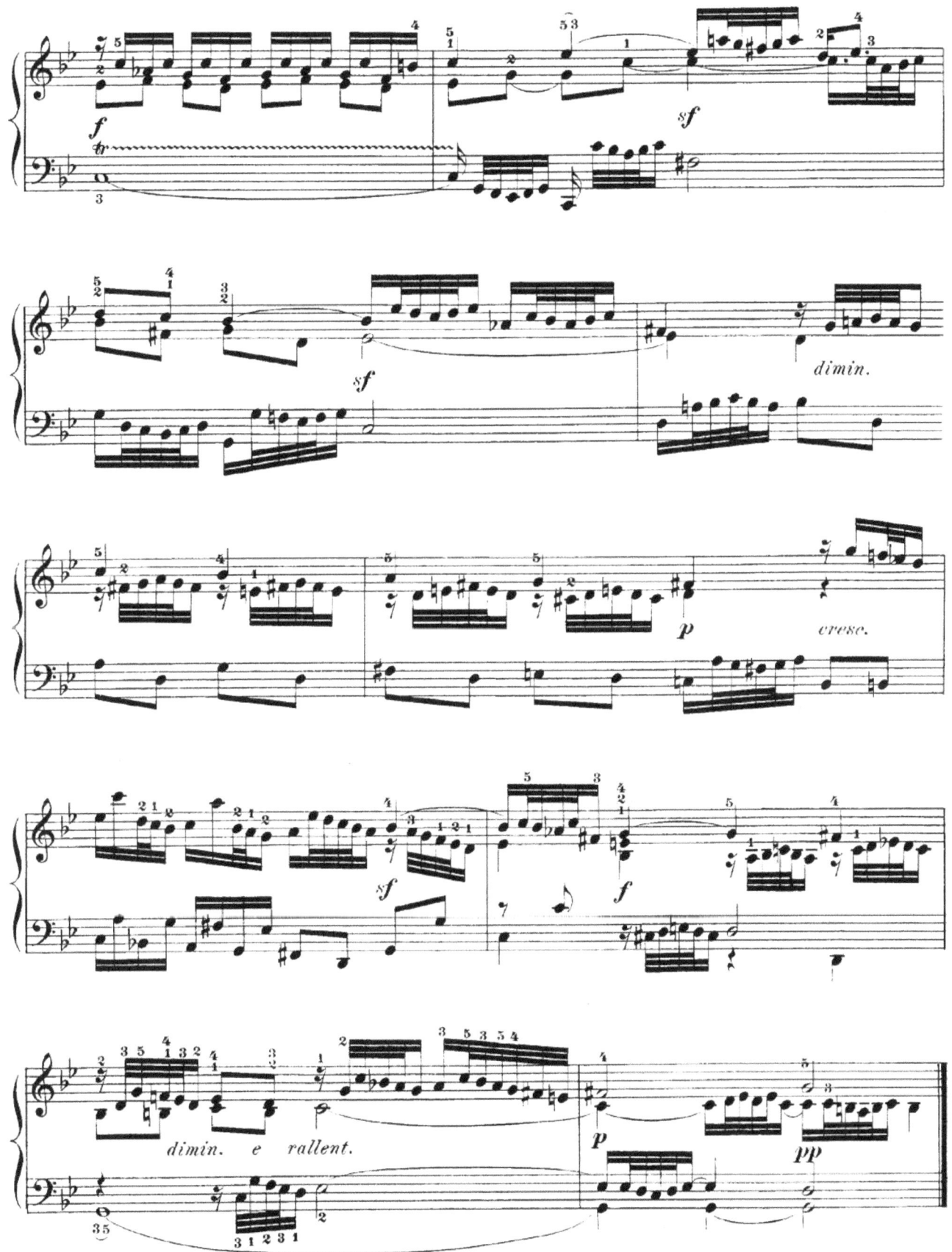

Fuga XVI.
a 4 Voci.

17. Prelude and Fugue in A-flat major BWV 862

Preludio XVII.

Fuga XVII.
a 4 Voci.

18. Prelude and Fugue in G-sharp minor BWV 863

Preludio XVIII.

103

Fuga XVIII.
a 4 Voci.

105

19. Prelude and Fugue in A major BWV 864

Preludio XIX.

Fuga XIX.
a 3 Voci.
Allegro moderato. (♩. = 69.)

20. Prelude and Fugue in A minor BWV 865

Preludio XX.

Fuga XX.

a 4 Voci.

Fuga XX.

a 4 Voci.

120

21. Prelude and Fugue in B-flat major BWV 866

Preludio XXI.

Fuga XXI.
a 3 Voci.

125

22. Prelude and Fugue in B-flat minor BWV 867

Preludio XXII.

Fuga XXII.
a 5 Voci.

130

23. Prelude and Fugue in B major BWV 868

Preludio XXIII.

133

Fuga XXIII.
a 4 Voci.

135

24. Prelude and Fugue in B minor BWV 869

Preludio XXIV.

Fuga XXIV.
a 4 Voci.

144